What's the Issue?

WHAT'S CLIMATE CHANGE?

By Robert M. Hamilton

KidHaven
PUBLISHING

Published in 2018 by
KidHaven Publishing, an Imprint of Greenhaven Publishing, LLC
353 3rd Avenue
Suite 255
New York, NY 10010

Designer: Seth Hughes
Editor: Katie Kawa

Photo credits: Cover (top), p. 15 FloridaStock/Shutterstock.com; cover (bottom) Tatiana Grozetskaya/Shutterstock.com; p. 4 Denis Burdin/Shutterstock.com; p. 5 MarcelClemens/Shutterstock.com; p. 6 DurkTalsma/iStock/Thinkstock; p. 7 Mario Tama/Getty Images; p. 8 PHILIPPE DESMAZES/AFP/Getty Images; p. 9 puttsk/Shutterstock.com; p. 10 David De Lossy/Photodisc/Thinkstock; p. 11 Mark Wilson/Getty Images; p. 12 stevanovicigor/iStock/Thinkstock; p. 13 David McNew/Getty Images; p. 14 S_Lew/iStock/Thinkstock; p. 16 LobodaPhoto/iStock/Thinkstock; p. 17 daulon/Shutterstock.com; p. 18 Photoslash/iStock/Thinkstock; p. 19 Scott Eisen/Getty Images; p. 20 scyther5/iStock/Thinkstock; p. 21 nesrin ozdemir/Shutterstock.com.

Library of Congress Cataloging-in-Publication Data

Names: Hamilton, Robert M., 1987- author.
Title: What's climate change? / Robert M. Hamilton.
Description: New York : KidHaven Publishing, [2018] | Series: What's the issue? | Includes bibliographical references and index.
Identifiers: LCCN 2017036563 (print) | LCCN 2017039872 (ebook) | ISBN 9781534524323 (eBook) | ISBN 9781534525009 (6 pack : alk. paper) | ISBN 9781534524316 (library bound book : alk. paper) | ISBN 9781534524996 (pbk. book : alk. paper)
Subjects: LCSH: Global warming–Juvenile literature. | Climatic changes–Juvenile literature. | Global environmental change–Juvenile literature.
Classification: LCC QC981.8.G56 (ebook) | LCC QC981.8.G56 H354 2018 (print) | DDC 363.738/74–dc23
LC record available at https://lccn.loc.gov/2017036563

Printed in the United States of America

CPSIA compliance information: Batch #CW18KL: For further information contact Greenhaven Publishing LLC, New York, New York at 1-844-317-7404.

Please visit our website, www.greenhavenpublishing.com. For a free color catalog of all our high-quality books, call toll free 1-844-317-7404 or fax 1-844-317-7405.

CONTENTS

A Hot Topic

Did you know Earth is getting warmer? Scientists are working hard to study the reasons why. They often talk about the warming of the planet—also known as global warming—as being part of something called climate change.

Climate is the weather in a certain place over a long period of time. Weather changes often, but climate doesn't. This is why it makes the news when the climate starts to change. Why is climate change happening, and what can we do about it? Read on to find out!

Facing the Facts 🔍

Between 1880 and 2017, Earth's temperature had gone up 1.7 degrees Fahrenheit (1 degree Celsius).

When the global climate changes, it **affects** all life on Earth. This is why it's important to understand climate change and what can be done to fight it.

Global Climate

When some people talk about climate, they talk about the climate of one part of the world. For example, the Sahara Desert's climate is hot and dry. This is called regional climate.

When people talk about climate change, however, they often talk about the climate of the whole planet. This is called global climate. Climate change affects the entire world—not just certain parts of it. When something changes in one part of the world, it changes things all over Earth. People who study global climate study things such as temperatures, sea levels, and **extreme** weather events around the world.

Facing the Facts 🔍

A climatologist is a person who studies climates and how they change.

Scientists also study glaciers, or large bodies of slowly moving ice, to learn about global climate change. Melting glaciers are an important sign of global warming.

Why Worry Now?

Climate change is not a new thing for our planet. In fact, Earth's climate has changed many times throughout history. There have been periods of time when much of the planet was covered with ice. These periods were called ice ages. After an ice age, the planet would warm up.

Why do people seem more worried about climate change now? Scientists believe Earth's climate is changing more quickly than it ever has before. They also believe this period of climate change—unlike the ones before—was caused by people.

ice core

The valleys in Montana's Glacier National Park, shown here, were formed by glaciers. There are still active, or moving, glaciers in the park. However, scientists fear those may melt because of climate change.

Facing the Facts

Scientists use ice cores—ice taken from glaciers by drilling—to study past climates. Snow and ice build up over the years, and each **layer** shows what the air, or atmosphere, was like at different times in history.

9

Too Much Water

Some glaciers have stayed on Earth even after the last ice age ended. These glaciers are melting as Earth's temperature is getting warmer. When a glacier melts, it turns to water, which is being added to bodies of water around the world. This is causing sea levels to rise.

Sea levels are also rising because every part of Earth, including its oceans, is getting warmer, and water **expands** as it warms. Rising sea levels can cause flooding along coasts. If nothing is done to stop rising sea levels, major cities could end up underwater!

Facing the Facts

Over the last 20 years, sea levels have risen by an average of 0.13 inch (3.3 mm) per year. That's about twice as fast as sea levels had risen in the previous 80 years.

Rising sea levels have led to flooding in many coastal cities around the world, including Washington, D.C.

Weird Weather

Because climate and weather are connected, it makes sense that changes in climate would cause changes in weather. Scientists are still studying how much of a part global warming has played in changing weather patterns.

There's scientific proof, though, that climate change has led to more and hotter heat waves around the world. The total amount of global **precipitation** has also increased. In addition, many scientists believe there's a connection between the climate getting hotter and storms getting stronger. If Earth's temperature gets hotter, heat waves and extreme weather events are expected to happen more often.

It's not always easy to tell how much climate change is affecting the weather. However, scientists do believe there's a connection between a warmer Earth and more extreme weather.

Facing the Facts

Scientists believe global warming could cause stronger **hurricanes** in the future. Rising sea levels could also make hurricanes more deadly.

Affecting Animals

Climate change isn't just affecting people. It's also affecting animals. As oceans get warmer and sea levels rise, animals' **habitats** are changing or disappearing. This affects how they live and find food.

For example, polar bears hunt on arctic sea ice. They can live on land for periods of time, but the ice is where they hunt most of their **prey**. As this ice continues to melt because of global warming, polar bears are quickly losing their habitat and need to find new ways to get food.

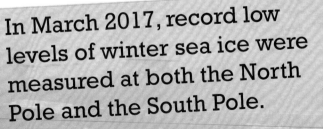

Facing the Facts

In March 2017, record low levels of winter sea ice were measured at both the North Pole and the South Pole.

Climate change is a
danger to animals
such as polar bears.

15

The Cause of Climate Change

What's causing Earth's climate to change so quickly? The main cause is human activity—mainly the burning of **fossil fuels**, such as coal and oil. These fuels power our homes, cars, airplanes, and factories, but they also make the planet hotter. This is because of the greenhouse effect.

In a greenhouse, warmth from the sun gets trapped by the glass, which makes the building hot. The same thing is happening on Earth. Burning fossil fuels causes certain gases, such as carbon dioxide, to build up in the atmosphere. These gases trap the sun's warmth, which makes the planet hotter.

THE GREENHOUSE EFFECT

energy going
back into space

heat trapped by
Earth's atmosphere

Facing the Facts

Trees take in carbon dioxide and keep it from getting into the atmosphere. However, when trees are cut down and burned to clear land for homes and farms, even more carbon dioxide is put into the air.

A Different Point of View

Scientific facts all point to climate change being a real problem and people being the main cause of it. However, some people still say that climate change isn't happening. Others may agree that the global climate is changing, but they believe it's a natural **process** that people don't have a **responsibility** to fix.

Many people who think this way don't want the government to make them lower the amount of the greenhouse gases they put in the air. They would rather say climate change isn't happening than change their way of life to try to fight it.

Some people argue that cold winters or strong winter storms are signs that global warming isn't really happening. However, science says otherwise.

Facing the Facts

Less than 50 percent of Americans said they worried "a great deal" about global warming in 2017, according to a **Gallup poll**. However, that number was still almost 10 percent higher than it was the year before.

19

Everyone Can Help!

Even though some people may not believe climate change is real, it's a fact that Earth is getting warmer. Rising sea levels, strong storms, and deadly heat waves may seem scary and hard to stop. However, there's work being done around the world to fight against global climate change.

World leaders have signed agreements to lower the amount of carbon dioxide put into the atmosphere. Inventors are creating cars that don't need fossil fuels. Even kids can help! Climate change may be a big problem, but every small action counts in the fight against it.

Facing the Facts

A person's carbon footprint is the amount of carbon dioxide put into the atmosphere because of their activities and energy needs.

WHAT CAN YOU DO?

Walk or ride a bike instead of taking a car.

Turn off lights and electronics when you're not using them.

Write to your U.S. Senators or members of the House of Representatives about the importance of fighting climate change.

Grow your own fruits and vegetables.

Plant trees.

Ask if you can start an environmental club or conservation club at school.

Recycle.

These are just some of the things you can do right now to help fight against climate change. You're never too young to make a difference!

GLOSSARY

affect: To produce an effect on something.

expand: To become bigger.

extreme: More than what is expected.

fossil fuel: A fuel, such as coal, oil, or natural gas, that is formed in the earth from dead plants or animals.

Gallup poll: A sample of the public's opinion on an issue taken by questioning a group of people meant to represent a certain population.

habitat: The natural home for plants, animals, and other living things.

hurricane: A tropical storm with strong winds, rain, thunder, and lightning.

layer: One part of something lying over or under another.

precipitation: Water that falls to the ground as hail, mist, rain, sleet, or snow.

prey: An animal hunted by other animals for food.

process: A series of actions or changes.

responsibility: Something a person must take care of or be in charge of.

FOR MORE INFORMATION

WEBSITES

Climate Kids: NASA's Eyes on the Earth
climatekids.nasa.gov
Visitors to this website will find helpful information about climates, climate change, and what kids can do to reduce their carbon footprint.

What Is Climate Change?
www.natgeokids.com/au/discover/geography/general-geography/what-is-climate-change
This website answers common questions about climate change in a way that is easy to understand.

BOOKS

Enz, Tammy. *Dynamic Planet: Exploring Changes on Earth with Science Projects*. North Mankato, MN: Capstone Press, 2016.

Mack, Molly. *Reducing Global Warming*. New York, NY: PowerKids Press, 2017.

Royston, Angela. *What Happens When an Ice Cap Melts?* Mankato, MN: Smart Apple Media, 2016.

INDEX